Making

D0861460

How to Cook Like a Mountain MeMa

by Lois Sutphin
an Authentic Mountain MeMa

FEB   2007

MAKING DO: HOW TO COOK LIKE A MOUNTAIN MEMA

by Lois Sutphin and Gina Farago
published by NeDeo Press

Copyright © 2005 by Lois Sutphin and Gina Farago

Cover Design and Illustrations by T. Glenn Bane
Cover Illustration by Kymberlee Goins
Cover Photography by Karl Farago
Interior Design and Layout by Terry Bane

ALL RIGHTS RESERVED

For information:
NeDeo Press
1 Terrace Way
Greensboro, NC 27403
www.NeDeoPress.com

ISBN 0-9763874-1-7

Library of Congress Control Number: 2005921086

Printed in the United States of America
1 3 5 7 9 0 8 6 4 2

Dedication

This book is dedicated to the
memory of Nellie Mae Sutphin,
my mother and the original
mountain MeMa.

—Lois Sutphin

Table of Contents

Making *Do*: Table of Contents

Preface

What is a mountain MeMa? Having been born and raised in the Blue Ridge Mountains of Virginia, the idea that someone might not know the answer to this question was peculiar to me. Everyone had a MeMa—the mother, the grandmother, the matriarch. She was the center of the family, its core, grown from a rich mountain heritage and rooted deep in the soil of its culture. Her strong hands could ring a chicken's neck for supper, then lovingly nurse an ailing friend back to health with a homemade poultice, its ingredients gathered from no farther away than the backyard. A MeMa could milk cows, wash clothes in the creek, and dress whatever came off the farm or out of the forest for a meal. She could raise one child or twelve, unflappably, while still tending to a husband and keeping a house, which she could clean in a minute. A MeMa, in short, could accomplish everything while possessing very little— she was the essence of making do.

This cookbook was born from that notion. I spent a lifetime watching my mother throw whatever was handy into a cooking pot, only for something wonderful to come out of it an hour later. I never figured out how she did it. It seemed too simple. Take what you have, throw in as much butter, sugar, or oil as you personally like or have available, simmer till done, and eat. All the cookbooks I've ever bought (and left dusty on a shelf) called for too much time and trouble. I never realized it, but the heart of "making do" was not just an old mountain way of cooking, but a method that could apply to even busy city lifestyles like mine.

I sat down with my mother—coauthor and a mountain MeMa—to capture this concept on paper. We blended the quickest and easiest recipes (like Old-Fashioned Skillet Cornbread) with a good mix of old-timey favorites that take a little more effort but are definitely worth the work (Molasses and Apple Butter Cake comes to mind). And all the recipes in this book are from scratch, just like the way real MeMas up on the Blue Ridge did it back then and, I'm sure, even today.

In compiling these recipes and vignettes from MeMa's childhood, I discovered that writing a cookbook based on the making do principle would be more of a challenge than I'd thought. Simple cooking gets complicated when "just throw in as much sugar as you want" needs to be narrowed down to an actual amount. We did it the best we could, but bear in mind if you make a recipe and would like it sweeter, saltier, spicier, or less of those things, by all means, adjust the recipe. That's what making do like an authentic mountain MeMa is all about.

—Gina Farago

About the Authors

Lois was born in 1934 at the Sutphin family's Old Home Place (pictured on the cover). Tucked amid the folds of the Blue Ridge Mountains, the small community of Laurel Fork, VA, was Lois's home for 48 years. She now resides in Robbins, NC, where her mountain recipes still grace the dinner table. This book is dedicated to Nellie Mae Sutphin, Lois's mother and the MeMa from which most of these recipes originated. Gina Farago is Lois's youngest daughter and a novelist. She lives with her husband, Karl, in Greensboro, NC, and has recently learned to cook thanks to the work involved in compiling this book.

Acknowledgments

A lot of these recipes came more from memory than a recipe box, and I sometimes needed a little help with recollection. Here's a big thank you to these folks for their time and trouble: Gaynelle Davis, Mabel Glenn, Texie Price, and Pauline Williams. Also, a special thanks to my daughter Barbara Bane and my grandson's wife, Terry Bane, for assisting Gina and me with the writing and editing of this book.

—*Lois Sutphin*

Rise and Shine

Breakfast Rice

(serves 4)

What ya need:

2 cups water

½ cup rice

a dab of salt

⅔ cup milk

1 tablespoon butter

sugar to taste

What ya do:

Heat 2 cups of water to a rolling boil. Add rice and the dab of salt. Lower heat, cover, and let rice boil slowly for 30-45 minutes until rice is mushy. When done, add milk, butter, and sugar. Serve in a bowl and enjoy!

Brown Milk Gravy
(serves 2)

What ya need:

6 strips of bacon or 4 sausage patties or 4 strips of fat
    back
1-2 tablespoons flour
salt and pepper to taste
2 cups milk (there'bouts)

What ya do:

Fry bacon, sausage, or fatback till done. Take out of frying pan. Stir flour into grease to thicken it to your liking.
Brown it, stirring constantly. Add salt and pepper. Then
add your milk and stir until it is boiling. It will thicken as it
boils. (Add more milk if gravy seems too thick.) Serve as
a side dish or pour over MeMa's Old-Timey Biscuits.

Preserving Breakfast Memories

Up on the mountain, we canned our morning sausage, just like tenderloin, fruit, and much of the other food we ate. The meat came straight off one of our farm's hogs, and as we had no freezer, canning was a way to preserve pork for meal after meal. First, the sausage was fried on the stove, then put in fruit jars with its own grease. All you had to do at breakfast was open up a jar, warm up the sausage, and make the brown milk gravy in the grease we'd saved. We kept the canned sausage in our cellar at room temperature, and it would last up to two years!

Buckwheat Pancakes
(makes about 8)

What ya need:

1 cup buckwheat flour

1 tablespoon baking powder

$1/4$ teaspoon salt

1 egg

1 cup milk

What ya do:

Sift together the flour, baking powder, and salt. In a separate bowl, beat the egg with the milk. Add slowly to the flour mixture. Beat until the large lumps disappear. Batter will be thin. Pour batter, about $1/4$ cup for each pancake, onto a hot griddle greased with butter. Cook until golden brown and then flip. When done, serve immediately with butter and syrup, or spread with molasses for a tasty alternative!

Buckwheat Harvesttime

We grew our own buckwheat each year. Planting season meant a lot of work, even for us young'uns. We planted the seed in the spring, and in the summer, the fields would be snowy with buckwheat bloom, lacy white and smelling like honey. The crops buzzed with honeybees working the blossoms.

When the buckwheat was ready, the threshing machine came in to harvest the field. A water-powered mill ground the buckwheat into flour (which Mama would use to cook up pancakes). When the flour was ready, my brother and I would put it on our backs, about half a bushel apiece, and tote it a mile home through the woods. I was 10.

Growing up, I can't say I looked forward to harvesttime, but, boy, I sure did look forward to those buckwheat pancakes afterwards.

Fried Cornbread Pancakes
(makes about 6)

What ya need:

1/2 cup plain cornmeal

1/2 cup plain flour

1 teaspoon baking powder

1/2 teaspoon baking soda

1/2 teaspoon salt

1 egg, well beaten

3/4 cup buttermilk

1/4 cup honey or 1 tablespoon sugar to sweeten batter

What ya do:

Mix all the ingredients. Grease griddle with shortening and heat on low. Pour the batter onto the griddle, allowing about 1/4 cup per pancake. Fry the pancakes till golden brown on each side. Serve with honey, syrup, or a mountain favorite, molasses.

Grape Juice
(2-3 gallons of grapes = 1 gallon of juice)

What ya need:

blue grapes (any kind will do)

sugar to taste

What ya do:

Put the grapes, skins and all, in a pot and cover just to their tops with boiling water. Let the grapes simmer on the stove until soft. Strain the grapes by mashing juice through a cloth. Put the juice in a cool place and strain again in 24 hours. Add sugar to sweeten to your liking and chill.

Fox Grapes

Store-bought grapes were a luxury growing up, and thank goodness we didn't need them. The nearest store only carried these "specialty fruits" at Christmastime, when they became a wonderful surprise in my stocking. But that didn't help at all when it was grape-juice-making time. So, as a child, I'd go into the woods behind our house and gather them wild, what we called fox grapes. Fox grapes were kindly sour and about as big around as a nickel. But they made some fine grape juice (and wine too!).

Mackerel and Eggs
(serves 6-8)

What ya need:
1 tablespoon butter

4 eggs, beaten

salt and pepper to taste

1 (14.75 ounces) can mackerel

What ya do:
Melt butter in a hot skillet and add eggs. Coarsely scramble the eggs (in larger chunks) until completely done. Add salt and pepper. Drain the mackerel and add to the eggs. Stir together until mackerel is warmed through.

Tasty Tidbit: Pretty darn good as a sandwich, too!

Tomato Juice

(½ bushel tomatoes = 1¼ gallons of juice)

What ya need:
fresh whole tomatoes
salt
honey or sugar to taste

What ya do:
Wash tomatoes and cut off the ends. Chop the tomatoes into coarse chunks. Simmer in a pot on low heat with
just enough water to cover, stirring often to keep from
sticking. Press tomatoes through a sieve when they are
tender and done. Stir in salt (1 teaspoon per quart) and
honey or sugar to taste. Chill.

Tip: If you want to can any leftover juice, the added salt
in the juice not only gives extra flavor, it also acts as a
preservative to keep the juice from spoiling.

Tomato Laurels

In the mountains, you get a lot of cold wind and late frosts, which are rough on vegetables, particularly young tomatoes. To shelter growing plants, we'd break off laurel branches and stick them in the ground around the tomatoes. The laurel leaves blocked the wind and kept the vegetables warm. When the tomatoes took root and started to grow, we could take the laurel branches away.

Notes

Our Daily Bread

Cornbread Cake

(serves 6-8)

What ya need:

1 cup self-rising flour

1/2 cup plain cornmeal

1/4 teaspoon baking soda

2 heaping tablespoons sugar

1 egg, beaten

1/2 cup buttermilk

1/2 cup water

What ya do:

Combine dry ingredients. Mix in remaining ingredients. Pour into a greased skillet and bake at 475 degrees for 20 minutes.

Cracklin' Bread

(serves 6)

What ya need:

1 cup plain cornmeal

1/4 teaspoon baking soda

1/4 teaspoon salt

1 heaping tablespoon baking powder

1/2 cup flour

1 egg

2 tablespoons sugar

1/2 cup buttermilk

1 cup cracklings

What ya do:

Mix ingredients and stir in cracklings. Pour into a greased pan and bake in a 450-degree oven till done, about 30 minutes. (Best if baked in an iron skillet.)

Tidbit: What is a cracklin' anyway? Render out the fat just inside pork ribs. Cut the fat into strips and fry them. A dried, fried fat strip is a cracklin'.

Daddy's Hoecake
(1 hoecake or 4 servings)

What ya need:

⅓ cup butter

1½ cups self-rising flour

1 teaspoon baking powder

1 cup milk

What ya do:

Melt butter in an iron skillet. Mix the other ingredients well and pour into the melted butter. Cook over medium-low heat until brown. Turn hoecake over one time.

Homemade White Bread
(makes 2 loaves)

What ya need:

8 cups plain flour

3 tablespoons sugar

2 packs of yeast

2 cups warm water

lard or butter

What ya do:

Combine 2 cups of flour, sugar, and yeast in a large bowl. Add in the warm water and beat 2 minutes. Work 1 cup of flour into dough. Then work in 5 more cups of flour, 1/2 cup at a time, until the dough is soft. Dump the dough onto a floured surface and knead until it has a satiny, elastic texture. Place in a greased bowl and grease top of dough with lard or butter. Cover and let rise in a warm place for about 1 1/2 hours. Dough will double in size. Punch down the dough and divide in half. Place the halves in separate loaf pans and press out any air bubbles. Let rise again (uncovered) until size is doubled, about 45 minutes. Bake at 375 degrees for about 30 minutes. Remove from pans to cool.

MeMa's Old-Timey Biscuits
(makes 8)

What ya need:

2 cups all-purpose flour

1 1/2 tablespoons baking powder

1/4 teaspoon baking soda

1 teaspoon salt

1 teaspoon sugar

3/4 cup buttermilk

1/3 cup lard (or shortening)

2 tablespoons butter (plus a few dabs as toppings)

What ya do:

Preheat oven to 450 degrees. Sift the dry ingredients into a bowl. Make a well in the center and pour in the buttermilk. Drop the lard and butter into the buttermilk and knead in the dry ingredients until dough makes a ball. Roll out dough on a lightly floured surface. Cut out the biscuits with a biscuit cutter and place on greased baking pan. Top each biscuit with a dab of butter. Bake for 10–12 minutes until lightly browned. Remove from oven and top again with a dab of butter.

Thunder Biscuit!

Mama was afraid of thunderstorms. If one came up at suppertime, she wouldn't let us eat until it had blown over. She'd make us kids sit real still and quiet—it didn't matter if it took till midnight for the storm to go. I never could figure out why Mama was bent on saving us from thunder and lightning inside the house!

In later years, when a storm rolled through, my phone would ring and Mama would call for my daughter to come sit the night with her. In the morning, she'd make her granddaughter hot homemade biscuits topped with a rich mix of Karo syrup and butter. To this day, biscuits, syrup, and butter remind me of Mama and a clear morning after a storm.

Brown-Sugar Breakfast

We never took breakfast treats for granted, my brothers and I, particularly not anything that came from the store. Although brown sugar was cheap, even back then it was special to us because we mostly ate what we had— meaning whatever we grew, shot, or trapped—and that often did not include store-bought items.

A trip to the store meant a mile-or-two trek through the woods and a couple of cow pastures, and we only had our feet or Daddy's old horse to carry us about. (Only one distant neighbor had a car, but he poked around in it so slow, it was quicker just to walk where you needed to go.)

It took some effort to get a box of brown sugar, but sprinkled atop Mama's old-timey biscuits, sticky with melted butter, made it well worth the trouble.

Old-Fashioned Skillet Cornbread
(serves 6-8)

What ya need:

1 cup plain cornmeal

1/2 cup plain flour

1 1/2 tablespoons baking powder

1 teaspoon salt

1 teaspoon baking soda

1/2 cup buttermilk

1/2 cup water

1 egg, beaten

1/4 cup melted lard or shortening

What ya do:

Combine the dry ingredients well, then mix in the buttermilk, water, and egg. Melt the lard or shortening in a cast-iron skillet. Pour batter into the greased skillet. Bake cornbread at 475 degrees for 20-25 minutes.

Tasty Tidbit: Pour milk in a glass, about 2/3 full. Crumble cold cornbread into the glass, then mix and eat. Yum!

Zucchini Bread

(makes 2 loaves)

What ya need:

3 cups flour

1 1/2 teaspoons salt

1 1/2 teaspoons baking soda

1/2 teaspoon baking powder

1 tablespoon cinnamon

1 1/4 cups lard (or oil)

2 1/2 cups sugar

4 eggs, beaten

4 cups zucchini, coarsely chopped

1/2 cup walnuts

1 cup golden raisins

What ya do:

Mix together flour, salt, baking soda, baking powder, and cinnamon. Set aside. Then mix together lard (oil), sugar, eggs, and zucchini. Add in the mixture of dry ingredients, plus the walnuts and raisins. Beat well. Pour into loaf pans and bake in a 325-degree oven for 50 minutes to 1 hour.

Notes

Odds and Ends

Apple Butter
(makes 1 quart)

What ya need:

9 medium tart apples, peeled and sliced thin

1/2 teaspoon cinnamon

1/2 teaspoon allspice

1/2 teaspoon nutmeg

1/2 teaspoon ground cloves

1/2 cup water

1 cup sugar

What ya do:

Use a stovetop pot with a heavy bottom, like copper. Put in apples, spices, and water. Cook slowly on low heat until apples are a smooth consistency. Add sugar, stirring constantly until apple butter reaches the desired color. (The sugar darkens the color as it cooks.)

Tasty Tidbit: Add more cloves if you like it spicy.

Blackberry Jelly

What ya need:

2 quarts fresh blackberries

1/3 cup water

1 cup sugar to 1 cup juice

What ya do:

Pick and wash your blackberries, and place in a pot. Add 1/3 cup of water to berries and bring to a boil. Cook 5 minutes. Let the berries cool. Put the berries in a clean cotton cloth. Make a bag and squeeze out the juice slowly back into the pot. Add 1 cup of sugar for every cup of juice. Boil the juice and sugar slowly. The juice will boil down to about half. The juice is ready when it drips slowly from a spoon. Pour into jars while hot. Jelly will thicken as it cools.

Fried Fatback

What ya need:
fatback

What ya do:
Slice fatback into strips about ¼ inch wide. Fry over low to medium heat until all grease has fried out of the meat and the strips are light brown. Remove from grease and drain.

Tasty Tidbit: Fatback is a staple of mountain cooking. Fried, it's a flavorful side dish while its grease seasons vegetables and substitutes for bacon or sausage when making brown milk gravy. Save any unused grease for future use by pouring into a jar and storing in the refrigerator.

Grape Wine

What ya need:
blue grapes
5 pounds sugar to 5 gallons juice
1 pack of yeast ($^1\!/_4$ ounce)

What ya do:
Put the grapes in a stoneware crock. Put a clean cloth
over the top. Let ferment 7-9 days. Then strain. Put the
juice back in the crock. Add sugar (5 pounds to every 5
gallons). Add 1 package of yeast to every 5 gallons of
juice. Let it work for 14 days. When it stops bubbling,
strain the juice into bottles or jars. Let sit for 1 day, then
strain the juice again. Repeat each day until there is no
sediment in the bottom.

Ketchup
(makes 1 pint)

What ya need first:

1 quart sliced tomatoes

1/3 cup chopped onion

1/2 teaspoon salt

a dab of pepper

What ya do first:

Simmer all the ingredients in water to cover till the tomatoes and onions are done (soft). Let cool. Then press through a sieve.

What ya need second:

1/2 teaspoon cinnamon

1/2 teaspoon cloves

1/3 cup vinegar

sugar or honey to taste

What ya do second:

Put the spices in a clean cotton cloth and tie it. Place in vinegar and simmer a few minutes. Remove spices and add spiced vinegar to tomato mixture. Boil rapidly, stirring constantly for 10 minutes or till slightly thickened. For sweet ketchup, add sugar or honey to taste.

Real Honest-to-Goodness Butter
(makes about ³/₄–1 pound)

What ya need:

2 pints heavy cream
½ teaspoon salt

What ya do:

Pour cream into a bowl and cover. Let warm to room temperature. If you don't have an hour to spare for churning,
use an electric mixer, on high, to mix until cream is thick
and fluffy. (Takes about 10 minutes.) Lower mixing
speed as needed, and continue to beat whipped cream
until it reduces to a watery consistency and buttery
clumps begin to form. Remove the butter clumps from the
milk. Rinse and knead the clumps under cold running
water until the water runs nearly clear. Knead salt into the
butter and refrigerate.

Tip: Pack the butter in a butter printer and turn it out
onto a saucer to make a pretty addition to your table at
suppertime.

Churning Up a Mean Temper

When I was a child, I hated to churn. And that was one of my jobs. What I knew most about churning was this: sitting on the porch in the summertime working that paddle—they called it a dash—up and down, up and down, up and down.

The milk to make the butter we churned had to come from somewhere, and when you lived in the country, that somewhere was done in the barn with four legs and an attitude. Mama had a cow in particular that we children dreaded like the switch. She could kick a kid right out of his shoes. Mama bought Daisy because her breed produced a lot of milk, never mind we were too terrified of her to attempt to get it.

Eventually, Mama did outsmart the hateful bovine. First, she had Daddy build a special pen beside the pasture fence. We had kickers that fit on a cow's back legs, but used alone on Daisy, they didn't last long. So next Mama put her in the pen *and* ran a bar in front of her legs *and* put her in the kickers—finally, we had milk!

While Mama wrestled with Daisy in the mornings, my brother Junior and I tended to our own gentler cattle. (Our younger brother, Elmer, was too little at the time to help us out.) We strained the milk we collected to get the hair, or whatever dripped in it while we were milking, out. Then we'd put the milk in crocks and take it to the spring-house where the springwater kept the liquid cool. We drank the milk straight from the crocks —there were no pasteurizers then and nobody knew they should boil it. Raw milk with all the cream removed was called Blue John because it had a bluish cast to it.

Notes

Appetizers and Pickled Picks

Deviled Eggs
(makes 1 dozen)

What ya need:

6 large eggs

¼ teaspoon salt

¼ teaspoon pepper

½ teaspoon vinegar

1½ tablespoons mayonnaise

2 tablespoons sugar

paprika (optional)

What ya do:

Boil the eggs until well done (about 10 minutes). Peel and then cut lengthwise through the middle of each egg. Put yolks in a bowl, whites on a platter. Mash the yolks and add salt, pepper, vinegar, mayonnaise, and sugar. Mix well and spoon back into whites. Sprinkle with paprika.

Tidbit: Unsure if egg is hard-boiled? Remove one, place on the counter, and give it a spin. If it spins fast, fast, fast, it is done. If it sort of lopes in a circle, it is not.

Pickled Beets

(makes 1 ½ quarts)

What ya need:

6 pounds fresh beets

1 cup vinegar

1 ½ cups sugar

2 cups water

What ya do:

Trim the beet tops. Boil the beets (in enough water to cover them) until tender, about 2 ½-3 hours. Put in cold water and rub the peeling off. Then cut into slices or wedges and place in a pot. Mix vinegar, sugar, and 2 cups water, stirring until sugar dissolves. Pour over beets and bring to a boil. Refrigerate the beets in their juice.

Pickled Eggs
(makes 1 dozen)

What ya need:

1 dozen eggs

$\frac{3}{4}$ cup vinegar

1 cup sugar

water

What ya do:

Hard-boil the eggs. When done, peel the eggs and drop in a jar with vinegar and sugar. Then fill up the jar with water. Refrigerate and let set for 3-4 days before eating.

Tidbit: Use red food coloring to give your eggs color, or use pickled beet juice instead. If using the beet juice, add an additional $\frac{1}{4}$ cup of vinegar to the eggs.

Pickled Peaches
(makes about 4 quarts)

What ya need:
12 pounds tight-stone peaches
2 tablespoons salt per ½ gallon water
2 tablespoons vinegar per ½ gallon water
water (enough to cover peaches)
1 quart white vinegar
2 cups water
⅓ teaspoon salt
3 cups sugar
whole cloves

What ya do:
Wash the peaches and remove their skins. Leave peaches whole and immediately place in a salt-vinegar-water mixture to keep them from turning dark. In a pot, mix 1 quart white vinegar, 2 cups water, ⅓ teaspoon salt, and sugar. Bring to a boil, then add peaches and simmer 5 minutes. Put peaches in a large bowl or jar, add a few cloves, and refrigerate.

Salt Pickles
(makes 4 quarts)

What ya need:

small cucumbers, enough to fill 4 quarts

1/2 cup vinegar

1/2 cup plain salt

6 cups water

What ya do:

Wash cucumbers and set aside. Mix the vinegar, salt, and water. Bring to a boil. Pour over whole, unpeeled cucumbers and refrigerate.

Sweet Cucumber Pickles

(makes 4 quarts)

What ya need:

small cucumbers, enough to fill 4 quarts

water for boiling

½ cup plain salt (or to taste)

2 cups white vinegar

1 cup water

1½ cups sugar (or to taste)

What ya do:

Wash cucumbers and place unpeeled in a pot. Add water and salt. Bring to a boil and immediately remove cucumbers from salt water. Discard the salt water and put in the pot the vinegar and a cup of fresh water. Add sugar until you think cucumbers will taste sweet enough for you. Dissolve sugar well. Add the cucumbers and simmer until they have changed color (to a dull green). Refrigerate.

White Cheese
(Looks Like Cottage Cheese But It's Not!)

What ya need:
farm-fresh whole milk (non-homogenized)
a dab of salt
a dab of pepper
a dab of sugar

What ya do:
Let milk sit out at room temperature until it clabbers, or curdles, about 1 day. Sieve liquid through a strainer to remove the curds. Place the strainer of curds over boiling water and cook until they are a little firm. Then add salt, pepper, and sugar to taste. Ready to eat when cheese cools.

Yellow Squash Pickles
(makes 2-3 pints)

What ya need:

1 ½ cups sugar

1 cup vinegar

1 hot pepper

1 tablespoon salt

½ teaspoon alum

½ teaspoon turmeric

5 cups sliced squash (yellow or green)

1 onion, chopped

What ya do:

Combine sugar, vinegar, pepper, salt, alum, and turmeric. Bring to a boil. Add squash and onions. Bring to a boil again and then refrigerate.

Soups, Salads, and Some Other Stuff

Cole Slaw

(serves 4)

What ya need:

4 cups shredded cabbage, loosely packed

1/2 teaspoon salt

1/4 teaspoon black pepper

1 teaspoon vinegar

1/4 cup sugar

5 tablespoons mayonnaise

What ya do:

Mix together all ingredients. Refrigerate for 30 minutes before serving.

Dad's Potato Soup

(serves 2)

What ya need:

4 potatoes

1 onion, chopped

1/2 teaspoon salt or to taste

1/2 teaspoon pepper or to taste

1 1/2 cups milk

4 tablespoons butter

What ya do:

Peel potatoes and dice into small pieces. Add chopped
onion to potatoes, cover with water, and boil till done.
Drain liquid, and mash potatoes and onion with a fork.
Add salt, pepper, milk, and butter. Mix well and bring
back to a boil. Ready to eat after second boil.

Potato Salad

(serves 6)

What ya need:

6 medium-sized potatoes

1/2 cup butter

1 1/2 tablespoons evaporated milk

1 1/2 teaspoons salt

6 eggs

1/2 cup onion, chopped fine

1/2 cup sweet pickle, chopped

1 1/2 tablespoons prepared yellow mustard

2/3 teaspoon black pepper

What ya do:

Peel potatoes, cut in 1/4-inch slices, and boil in water till done. Drain off liquid. Mix in butter, milk, and salt. Mash until smooth. Meanwhile, boil eggs. Peel and chop them coarsely. Add to eggs the onion and sweet pickle, then pour into potatoes, along with the mustard and pepper. Mix well and chill.

Salad Peas
(serves 5-6)

What ya need:
2 quarts fresh sugar snap peas
2-inch square of fatback
1 teaspoon salt (optional)

What ya do:
Remove tips and strings and break peas as you would green beans. Put fatback in a pot with water to cover and boil until meat is almost done. Add peas and salt. (Leftover liquid should be just enough to barely cover peas. If fatback is salty, you may not need to add salt.) Cook slowly until done (almost dry).

Tip: Don't let peas get overcooked. They'll turn to mush that way!

Vegetable Soup
(serves 10)

What ya need first:

1 1/2 cups uncooked elbow macaroni

1/3 cup milk

salt to taste

butter to taste

2 cups green peas

2 cups whole kernel corn

What ya do first:

Boil the macaroni in water till tender. Drain, then add the milk, salt, and butter. Cook peas and corn separately till tender, also seasoning with salt and butter to taste. Set aside.

What ya need second:

5 medium potatoes

3 onions

2 cups shredded cabbage

1 tablespoon salt

butter or oil to taste

2 cups kidney beans, canned

2 quarts tomato juice

sugar to taste

What ya do second:

Dice potatoes and chop onions. Put them, along with the cabbage, in a pot with just enough water to cover and slow boil until tender. Add salt and enough butter to season to your liking. Cook down till almost dry (or drain). Add cooked macaroni, peas, corn, kidney beans, and tomato juice. Sweeten with sugar to taste and bring back to a boil.

Tasty Tidbit: Precooking and seasoning the vegetables fills them with flavor before they go into the soup.

Wilted Lettuce Salad

What ya need:
fresh garden lettuce
young onions with green blades
$\frac{1}{2}$ teaspoon salt
hot grease (best if from fatback)

What ya do:
Wash lettuce and onions (including the blades) and cut into small pieces. Toss with salt. Pour hot grease over the top and stir. Eat while grease is still hot.

Tasty Tidbit: May substitute hot vegetable oil or bacon grease for the fatback.

Notes

Everyday Supper Fare

Baked Beans
(serves 6-8)

What ya need:

6 slices bacon

bacon grease (saved over from frying bacon, up to
   1/4 cup)

3 1-ounce can pork and beans

1/2 cup finely chopped onion

1/2 cup finely chopped green pepper

1/2 cup ketchup

3 hot dogs

1/3 cup plus 2 tablespoons brown sugar

What ya do:

Fry the bacon crisp. Drain off grease to use later, and
let bacon cool on a paper towel. Meanwhile, mix together
the pork and beans, onion, and green pepper. Then stir
in the ketchup. Slice hot dogs into the mixture, add the
brown sugar, and stir again. Crumble the fried bacon and
mix into the beans, followed by the bacon grease for seasoning. Bake in a 400-degree oven for about 1 hour.

Beef Stew

(serves 4)

What ya need:

1 cup oil (or shortening)

1 pound stew beef with some fat

1 teaspoon salt

flour

2 cups water

$1/4$ teaspoon black pepper

5 medium potatoes, peeled and quartered

1 carrot, sliced thin

1 onion cut up

What ya do:

Heat oil in skillet over medium heat. Salt the meat (about $1/2$ teaspoon) and roll in flour until all sides are coated. Fry in the oil until brown. Remove and place in large cooking pot. Add 3 tablespoons flour to the oil remaining in the skillet; stir constantly until flour is browned. Add 2 cups water and stir until gravy is smooth. Pour over stew beef, and add more water if needed to cover beef about $1\frac{1}{2}$ inches. Add black pepper. Bring to a boil and then lower heat to simmer. Cover and cook about 1 hour and 15 minutes. Gravy should be thick. Add potatoes, carrots, onion, and another $\frac{1}{2}$ teaspoon salt. Bring back to boil, then lower to simmer until vegetables are tender, about 30 minutes. Stir occasionally.

Chicken and Dumplings
(serves 6-8)

What ya need:
1 whole chicken with a lot of fat on it
1/2 teaspoon salt
1/2 teaspoon pepper
1/2 cup butter
1 cup milk
biscuit dough (see "MeMa's Old-Timey Biscuits")

What ya do:
Cut up chicken and place in a pot. Add just enough water to cover. Add salt, pepper, and butter. When water starts to boil, turn heat down to medium-low and cook slowly, about 1 hour. When done, remove chicken pieces from broth. Add milk to broth and bring back to a boil. Drop spoonfuls of biscuit dough into broth, then let simmer till done. (Add a little more salt and pepper, if desired.)

Tip: For fluffy dumplings, do not stir while cooking.

Stuffed Chicken Breasts
(serves 4)

What ya need:

4 chicken breasts with skin

salt

chicken dressing (see "Chicken Dressing")

butter or margarine

pepper

What ya do:

Wash the breasts and pat dry. Lift the skin and sprinkle in ½ teaspoon salt. Stuff the uncooked chicken dressing under the skin of the breasts, as much as you can pack in. Rub the tops of the breasts with butter, salt, and pepper. Place in a baking pan with any leftover dressing. Cover lightly with foil. Bake in a 375-degree oven about 1½ hours or until done.

Chicken Dressing

(serves 6)

What ya need:

4 cups crumbled cornbread (see "Old-Fashioned
   Skillet Cornbread")

1 cup finely chopped onion

1 tablespoon sage (optional)

1 teaspoon black pepper

2 cups chicken broth (seasoned with salt, if desired)

gizzards and livers, cooked and chopped (optional)

butter (a few tablespoons)

What ya do:

Combine all the ingredients in a large bowl, except for
the butter. Put in a pan. Dot the top of the bread mixture
with butter. Bake at 400 degrees for 1-1 1/2 hours until
dry and brown.

How to Fix a Real Fresh Chicken

When we wanted to eat chicken, it meant a trip to the henhouse, not the grocery store. It was a gruesome task, killing the chicken, but this job always fell to Mama, not my father. She could wield an ax or ring a neck, but I never watched either way.

I remember one time when the chickens fought back. Our rooster flogged Mama on her way to the granary. It leaped on her back, pecking and spurring. Mama never cussed, in fact she could keep her composure through most any predicament, but she did promise that rooster she would "fix him, wait and see." The next night we had roasted rooster instead of hen for dinner.

Fried Chicken

What ya need:

1 whole chicken, cut into parts
salt and pepper
flour
butter
vegetable oil

What ya do:

Clean the chicken pieces by rinsing in cold water.
Liberally salt and pepper each piece and roll in the flour
to coat well. Put about equal amounts of butter and vegetable oil into your fry pan, enough to more than cover
the bottom of it (for example, $^2/_3$ cup butter and $^2/_3$ cup
oil, more or less depending on the size of your pan).
When the oil and butter start sizzling, put in the chicken.
Adjust the heat to a nice simmer. Keep checking the bottoms of the meat and flip when the pieces turn golden
brown. Continue checking and flipping chicken until all
pieces are golden brown and the meat is thoroughly
cooked (about 45 minutes to over an hour, depending on
size of chicken pieces).

Meat Loaf

(serves 8)

What ya need:

1 1/2 pounds ground chuck

1/2 cup chopped onion

8 ounces tomato sauce

1 egg

1 teaspoon salt

1 teaspoon pepper

1/2 cup ketchup (plus some extra for topping)

1 tablespoon sugar

2 hot dog buns (or 2 slices of frozen light bread)

What ya do:

Knead ground chuck in a bowl. Add the onion, tomato sauce, egg, salt, pepper, and ketchup and knead into the meat. Add the sugar and crumble the buns into the meat mixture. Knead all together again until well mixed and all bread is moist. Put meat in a loaf pan and pat the meat out to the edges. Smooth a very thin layer of ketchup over the meat and bake in a 400-degree oven for 1-1 1/2 hours.

Mountain-Style Western Beans
(serves 6)

What ya need:

6-8 strips bacon

1 pound ground beef

1 large onion, coarsely chopped

2 tablespoons mustard

$\frac{1}{4}$ cup ketchup

4 tablespoons Karo syrup (or 2 tablespoons molasses)

$\frac{1}{2}$ teaspoon salt

$\frac{1}{2}$ teaspoon pepper

1 teaspoon chili powder

1 can (15 ounces) pork and beans

1 can (15 ounces) kidney beans

What ya do:

Fry bacon brown in a deep skillet. Take it out of pan and put beef and onion in bacon grease. Brown completely and drain. Coarsely crumble bacon and add to beef and onion. Add the mustard, ketchup, syrup, salt, pepper, and chili powder and mix well. Then add in the beans. Bring the mixture to a boil, then lower heat and simmer for 30 minutes.

How to Shell Your Pintos

To shell dried pintos, other beans, or peas, put them in a bag and beat with a mallet. Or you can stomp on them. When you have the beans beat out, separate them from the hulls. Then place them in a hot oven on a shallow tray for 10-15 minutes. This will kill any insect eggs that might be on the beans if taken fresh from the garden. When the beans are cold, put them in a container with a tight lid for storage.

Pinto Beans and Ham

(serves 6-8)

What ya need:

1 pound dry pinto beans

$1/2$- to 1-pound ham hock

water

What ya do:

Soak your pintos overnight. Put the ham hock in a big pot and add water to cook in (about $2\frac{1}{2}$ quarts). Bring to a rolling boil, then turn down heat to a slow boil. Cook the meat until done (about $1\frac{1}{2}$ hours). Rinse the pinto beans and add to the meat pot. Bring to a slow boil again and cook for another 2 hours. If you want a thick soup with your beans and ham, mash some of the beans with a potato masher and let cook another $1/2$ hour.

Tasty Tidbit: Cooking the ham and pintos slowly allows the meal to retain more of its flavor. Believe it or not, by soaking your pintos overnight, you've speeded up your cook time!

Clarence
(Or Whatever Chunk of Meat You Got)

Growing up in the mountains, I realized the purpose of raising chickens, cows, and hogs was to provide us with food. Having them as pets was not a luxury afforded us. Seeing Mama behead a chicken, or a cow toted off to slaughter, or hearing the squeals of pigs from behind the hill at hog-killing time meant good food for our table. This only changed after the birth of my first daughter. My husband, Dan, and I continued to raise a pig each year for the meat. Our daughter would name him, play with him, and cry her eyes out whenever he went missing. We managed to keep from her the connection of the pig going to "live somewhere else" and the sausage, ham, and pork chops on our table.

Still, it began to bother us. The meat was not so good when you knew the name of the donor and that it had been loved by your little girl. The charade was over with Clarence, the last pig we ever raised and killed. All our meat afterwards came from the grocery store and was, at least to us, anonymous.

Pot Roast

(serves 6)

What ya need:

3-4 pounds rump roast (sirloin or other meat of your choice)

2 teaspoons salt

1/2 teaspoon black pepper

flour

1/3 cup grease (or vegetable oil)

water

8 medium potatoes, sliced or quartered

4 medium onions, chopped

1 large carrot, sliced thin

What ya do:

Rub both sides of meat with salt and pepper. Coat generously with flour. Put in a 6-quart pot with the grease (oil) and brown both sides of meat on low heat. When brown, add water till it just covers the meat. Simmer for about 2 1/2 hours. Add potatoes, onions, and carrot to the pot. Simmer until vegetables are tender. Gravy should be brown and thick.

Salmon Cakes

(makes 5 patties)

What ya need:

1 can salmon (14.75 ounces)

1 egg

1/4 cup milk

1 cup breadcrumbs

1/4 cup butter

1/4 cup oil

What ya do:

Drain salmon and combine with egg, milk, and bread-crumbs. Mix together until smooth and thick enough to stick together well (add more breadcrumbs as needed). Melt butter and oil in a hot skillet. Pat mixture into patties, place in the skillet, and fry on medium heat until both sides are brown.

Fried Salt Fish

What ya need:
salt fish
cold water
cornmeal
grease (vegetable oil) for frying

What ya do:
Soak the fish overnight in the water to remove some of the salt. Debone the fish, then roll in cornmeal and fry in the grease till brown.

Tidbit: Salt fish came to our old country stores in wooden barrels. They were about the size of my two hands spread out together. One fish would be enough for one person at a meal.

Souse Meat

What ya need:
hog's head

water

sage to taste

salt to taste

pepper to taste

What ya do:
Take the lower part of the hog's head (the jowls) and cover with water in a pot. Cook the water down low until meat is so tender it will fall off the bone. Remove the bone and excessive fat and grease. Season with sage, salt, and pepper to your taste. Run meat through a sausage grinder, then let it set up in a pan (or till meat gets cold).

Tomatoes and Macaroni

(serves 4)

What ya need:

1 cup uncooked elbow macaroni

1/2 teaspoon salt

1 tablespoon butter

canned tomatoes (16 ounces)

1 tablespoon flour

What ya do:

Cook macaroni by adding to boiling water, seasoned with salt and butter. When done, drain. Add tomatoes to macaroni, keeping out a little of the juice. Mix flour into juice and beat until smooth. Bring macaroni and tomatoes to a boil, and add in the juice-flour mixture. Stir till liquid thickens and serve.

Fried Trout

What ya need:
cleaned trout

cornmeal

salt to taste

grease (vegetable oil)

What ya do:
Split the fish down the middle and roll in cornmeal and salt. Fry in the hot grease till done.

Notes

Mountain Critter
Main Dishes

Huntin' Bullfrogs

My daddy and oldest brother were hunters, as most mountain men grew up to be in those days. They stalked deer, squirrels, bobcats, and, occasionally, bullfrogs. Now, there are some conventional methods of capturing bullfrogs for a meal, gigging with a pointy stick the most common. But Daddy and Junior preferred another way—they used rifles. Never mind that shooting toward water is a good way to put your eye out with a bullet ricochet. Daddy and Junior weren't concerned with such things. On a good night, they'd bag about eight unsuspecting frogs, then bring them home for Mama to clean and cook up. (And the stories are true—frog legs do jump around in the pan; the salt in the soaking water pulls the tendons, making them quiver.)

Daddy and Junior eventually gave up their frog-hunting days, however. They never cottoned to the idea of killing something for its legs and wasting the rest.

Frog Legs
(serves 4)

What ya need:
8 frog legs, fat and juicy
salt water
flour
oil

What ya do:
Soak the legs in salted water overnight. Wash well. Roll in flour and fry in oil until done, the same way you would fry a chicken.

Fried Possum

(serves 8)

What ya need:

1 fat possum

salt water

vinegar

flour

salt

pepper

grease (vegetable oil)

What ya do:

Skin and clean the possum, including removing the head, tail, and innards. Cut up into pieces, then soak in salt water and a little vinegar for a good 12 hours. Then put the meat in a pot of boiling water and boil until done (meat will be tender). Remove meat and roll in flour with a little salt and pepper added. Fry possum in grease until golden brown.

Tasty Tidbit: For the fattest, tastiest possum, feed it fresh fruit and grain for 10 days prior to dinnertime.

Roasted Possum

(serves 8)

What ya need:

1 fat possum
cooking oil
flour
whole sweet potatoes with skins

What ya do:

If roasting the possum whole, clean by taking off the head, tail, and feet. Rub well with cooking oil, then roll the meat in flour. Put in a roasting pan and let bake at 375 degrees for about 3 hours. In the meantime, bake the sweet potatoes. When the possum is ready, put on a serving platter and surround with the potatoes.

Tip: Possum is good to make on holidays because it serves so many. But remember! Remove the head and tail to dress the table up nicer. Nobody likes their dinner staring at them.

Quail
(serves 3)

What ya need:

6 quail, dressed

2 cups water for cooking

½ teaspoon salt

⅓ teaspoon pepper

2 heaping tablespoons butter

What ya do:

Soak quail in water until the blood is out of each breast. It'll take about a half hour. Then rinse off and, using only the breasts, put in a pot with 2 cups fresh water, salt, and pepper. Boil until done, at least 30 minutes. Season with butter and make gravy out of the broth (see "Quail Gravy"). Do not remove the quail when making the gravy.

Quail Gravy

What ya need:
broth from boiled quail (see "Quail")
1/2 cup milk (about)
1/4 cup flour
1/2 cup water

What ya do:
Add milk to broth and bring to a boil. Mix flour and water in a bowl. Beat till smooth, adding flour as necessary until you get the gravy thickness you want. Pour flour mixture into the pot with the broth and milk. Let gravy thicken to desired consistency over a low heat.

Gumming Rabbits

Rabbit traps were also known as gums, and my brothers and I each had one of our own. In the wintertime, we would set them in the woods and bait them with apples. In the morning, we couldn't wait to get to our traps to see if we'd caught anything. In snowy weather, we could follow tracks right up into the rabbit gums. While my brothers were not squeamish about "taking care" of their rabbits then and there, Daddy always had to trek out to the trap and get mine.

Fried Rabbit
(serves 3)

What ya need:
1 fat rabbit

flour

salt to taste

pepper to taste

grease (vegetable oil)

What ya do:
Skin and clean the rabbit, then cut up and put in cold water to soak several hours (until water runs clear when meat is rinsed). Put the meat in a pot and boil until it begins to get tender. Remove from boiling water and roll in flour, salt, and pepper. Fry rabbit slowly in grease until good and brown.

Tidbit: Always trap your rabbit in the cold season. Otherwise, you may accidentally kill a mother with young. By winter, all babies are grown and gone.

How to Select a Tasty Squirrel

Look for your squirrels in the fall when they're shiny and fat from a summer of eating. Also, their babies are grown and gone for the year, so there are no worries of leaving orphans.

Daddy's squirrel season would begin when he noticed the squirrels cutting in the hickory trees for nuts. "Cutting" meant when the squirrels looked for nuts and cut into them with their teeth.

Squirrel With Gravy
(serves 3)

What ya need:
1 fat squirrel

$\frac{1}{2}$ teaspoon salt

2 heaping tablespoons butter

$\frac{1}{2}$ cup milk

$\frac{1}{3}$ teaspoon pepper

2 tablespoons flour

water

What ya do:
Skin and clean the squirrel, then soak in water. Wash and rinse the squirrel several times until the water runs clear. Cut up the squirrel and put the pieces in a pot to boil with salt and butter. Then simmer until done. Take out of the pot and debone. Put back in the pot, adding milk and pepper. Bring to a boil again. Beat flour with a little water in a bowl until smooth. Pour into the pot with the boiling milk and broth. Stir until the gravy is thick enough for you.

Fried Turtle

(serves 10)

What ya need:

1 big mud turtle, shelled

water

2 tablespoons salt

1/3 cup vinegar

flour

salt to taste

pepper to taste

grease (vegetable oil)

What ya do:

Scrape turtle meat from the shell and skin the hind legs.
Discard the rest. Soak the meat in water with the salt
and vinegar added. (Soak until water runs clear when
meat is rinsed.) Boil the meat until done, about 3-4 hours;
it will be tender when stuck with a fork. Slice the meat
and roll in a mixture of flour, salt, and pepper. Fry in
grease until brown.

Venison

(serves 6)

What ya need:

4 pounds venison

water

1 cup white vinegar

1 teaspoon salt

flour

salt

pepper

grease (vegetable oil)

What ya do:

Cut the meat up as you would beef. Soak it overnight in water, vinegar, and salt. (Use enough water to thoroughly cover the meat.) Remove the venison and wash well. Cook as you would a pot roast (see the "Pot Roast" recipe). Thinly slice the meat when done, then roll in a flour, salt, and pepper mixture. Slowly fry in grease until both sides are brown.

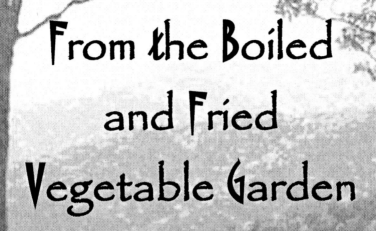

From the Boiled
and Fried
Vegetable Garden

Cabbage in a Furrow

In the country, we preserved our fruits and vegetables by canning, drying, or putting them in a hole in the ground. For cabbage, we plowed a furrow with a horse and put our cabbages in it. Then we covered them with dirt. They wouldn't keep very long, though; if not eaten quickly, they would taste like the soil. But our parsnips stayed in the ground all winter—freezing made them better.

Potatoes, turnips, and rutabagas were put in separate large holes in the ground. The holes were dug about four feet deep and covered with plank boards with dirt heaped over top. They would keep fresh all winter and would not freeze.

Boiled Cabbage
(serves 6)

What ya need:

2-inch square of fatback

1 medium cabbage head

1 teaspoon salt

1 teaspoon pepper

1 red pepper (optional)

What ya do:

Boil the fatback slowly for 2 hours in a medium pot about half full with water. Cut up the cabbage into large chunks. Put cabbage, salt, and pepper into the pot with the fatback. (Add the red pepper, if desired.) Boil again for about 20-25 minutes until the cabbage is tender when poked with a fork.

Fried Cabbage

(serves 4)

What ya need:

6 thin slices of fatback

½ cabbage head

½ teaspoon salt

½ teaspoon pepper

⅓ cup water

What ya do:

Fry the grease out of the fatback slices. Then take the slices out of the pan, leaving the grease. Finely chop the cabbage and put it into the grease. Add salt, pepper, and water. Cover with lid and fry slowly until done, about 30 minutes or until dry.

Corn Pudding
(serves 4-6)

What ya need:

2 cups corn (see Tip below)

2 eggs, well beaten

$1/2$ cup milk

2 tablespoons butter

$1/2$ teaspoon pepper

What ya do:

Combine corn, eggs, milk, butter, and pepper in a bowl. Mix thoroughly and pour into a well-greased baking dish. Bake at 400 degrees for about 45 minutes. When a knife inserted into the center comes out clean, pudding is done.

Tip: This recipe works best with cream corn made from fresh corn. Canned whole kernel corn that has been drained can be used as well.

Cream Corn

(serves 6)

What ya need:

8 ears of corn, fresh from the garden for best results

4 tablespoons butter

salt to taste

pepper to taste

What ya do:

Cut the corn off the ears. Then scrape the corncobs with a knife to get the remaining corn and corn "milk." Put the corn and corn milk in a pot with the butter, salt, and pepper. Bring it all to a boil and then simmer until thickened. Cooking time is about 30 minutes.

Tip: Store-bought unshucked corn may have a lower corn milk content than fresh corn from the garden. If your corn is not producing enough milk, add 1/2 cup evaporated milk and a tablespoon of cornstarch or flour, and follow the recipe above.

Green Beans
(serves 4-6)

What ya need:
2-inch square of fatback
3 quarts fresh green beans
$\frac{1}{2}$ teaspoon sugar or to taste
salt to taste

What ya do:
Boil fatback until the water has about boiled down to a fourth and the meat is almost done. Break and wash your beans, then put in the pot with the fatback, sugar, and salt. Bring to a boil. Immediately turn heat down to medium and simmer beans until dry (about 45 minutes to an hour).

Green Peas With Potatoes and Gravy
(serves 6)

What ya need first:

3 potatoes

1/2 teaspoon salt

2 tablespoons butter

What ya need second:

3 cups drained peas (see Tip on page 111 if using fresh
garden or frozen peas)

2 tablespoons sugar

1 cup evaporated milk

1/2 cup water

1/3 cup butter

1/8 teaspoon pepper or to taste

1/2 cup milk

1 tablespoon flour

What ya do:

Peel potatoes and slice in half-inch wedges. Put in a pot
along with the salt and butter. Pour in enough water to
cover the potatoes and boil until done (potatoes will be

tender when poked with a fork). Drain the potatoes and add in the peas, sugar, evaporated milk, and water. Mix all ingredients. Add butter and pepper, and mix again. In a separate bowl, combine milk and flour to make thickener for gravy. Bring potatoes and peas to a boil, then add thickener and stir about 3 minutes until the gravy is done. Turn off heat and eat.

Tip: If using peas from the garden or frozen peas, measure out 3 cups and cook them with the potatoes from the get-go.

Fried Green Tomatoes

(serves 4)

What ya need:

6 thin slices of fatback

6 (1/4-inch-thick) sliced green tomatoes

sugar

salt

black pepper

flour (enough to coat all tomatoes)

What ya do:

Fry the fatback till crisp, then remove from pan. Sprinkle each tomato slice with sugar, salt, and pepper. Roll tomato slices in flour. Put slices in fatback grease. Brown on both sides on medium heat, then cook on low until done (golden brown and soft when poked with a fork). Drain and enjoy!

Tasty Tidbit: We always liked to eat fried green tomatoes alongside cornbread covered in milk gravy. Rib-sticking good!

Hanovers (Rutabagas)

(serves 6-8)

What ya need:

1 pork shank

4 large hanovers, sliced medium thin

1/2 teaspoon salt

1/2 teaspoon pepper

1 tablespoon sugar

What ya do:

Boil the shank until done (meat will easily come off bone).
Add hanovers, salt, and pepper to the water with the
meat. Cook until almost done (starting to get tender) and
add sugar. Finish cooking till done.

Tasty Tidbit: Turnips can be cooked the same way!

Hominy

What ya need:

½ bushel shelled white hard-kernel corn

6-8 thin slices of fatback

salt to taste

What ya do first:

Put the corn in a large enamel, stainless steel, or glass pot full of cold water, and keep it cold for one day. Then cook the corn in the same water, adding 1 ounce (per gallon of water) of Red Devil Lye to loosen the husks. Keep stirring while cooking, straining the husks off the outside of the corn as it cooks. When corn is done, drain off the water and wash corn in clean water 4 times or more to make sure no traces of lye remain. (Warning: Lye is extremely poisonous. Do not accidentally eat it or breathe the fumes. Use caution when preparing this recipe the old-timey way, and read the directions on your lye package before using.)

What ya do second:

Fry fatback, then take out of the grease. Put your hominy in the grease and fry with a dab of salt. When food is well seasoned, it is ready to eat.

Tip: Red Devil Lye takes the husks off corn and the taste buds right off your tongue. Don't forget—rinse, rinse, rinse the lye from the corn before making the recipe. And keep children and pets away when handling this toxic substance!

Leather Britches (Dried Green Beans)
(makes 2 quarts)

What ya need:
1 quart dried green beans

2-inch square of thick fatback

1 teaspoon salt

1 small red hot pepper

What ya do:
Soak the green beans overnight before cooking. Drain. Boil fatback until about half done, then add in beans, salt, and hot pepper. Cook until beans are done. Very little liquid should be left in the pot (cook dry as you would green beans normally).

Tip: Whenever you soak anything dried, the amount will double!

How to Dry Your Leather Britches

First pick your green beans and string them. (We used white half-runners, and believe me, they have strings!) Don't break the beans; leave them whole. Then take a needle with strong thread and lace through the center of the beans until you have as many as you want on one strand. Make a loop on the end of the thread and hang the beans up in a dry place that is warm—we dried ours behind the wood cookstove. When they are dry, put the beans in closed containers so that bugs will not get in them. Store until you are ready to eat!

Mixed Turnip and Mustard Greens
(serves 4)

What ya need:
potful of turnip and mustard greens
6 thin slices of fatback

What ya do:
Clean and wash leaves carefully. Boil greens until done, then drain into a bowl. Cut them up. Meanwhile, fry fatback until done. Take out the meat and put greens in the grease. Fry slowly and until well seasoned (until greens have absorbed the grease).

Tip: Greens wither down next to nothing when cooked, so start with a whole potful!

Old-Fashioned Mashed Potatoes

(serves 6-8)

What ya need:

6 large peeled potatoes

1 teaspoon salt

1 cup butter

pepper to taste

2 tablespoons evaporated milk

What ya do:

Cut clean, peeled potatoes into chunks and boil in salted water until soft. Drain water and add butter, pepper, and evaporated milk. Mash with a potato masher until smooth.

Tip: Boiling potatoes in salted water flavors them while cooking.

Tasty Tidbit: Use any leftover mashed potatoes with the "Potato Cakes" recipe.

Fried Parsnips and Potatoes
(serves 4)

What ya need:

4 parsnips, peeled and thinly sliced

4 potatoes, peeled and thinly sliced

⅓ pound butter

½ teaspoon salt

½ teaspoon pepper

½ cup water

2 tablespoons sugar

What ya do:

Put parsnips and potatoes in a frying pan with butter, salt, and pepper. When they start frying, add the water. Fry slowly and stir often so they won't burn. When almost done, sprinkle with sugar. Then simmer till completely done (about 30-35 minutes).

Tasty Tidbit: Don't dig up your garden parsnips. Keep them in the ground until spring—winter freezing makes them better.

Boiled Parsnips

(serves 4-6)

What ya need:

2-inch square of fatback

6 medium parsnips, cut into chunks

1 tablespoon sugar

What ya do:

Boil fatback in a pot half full of water. When done, add the parsnips and boil again until they are done (about 30 minutes; water should be almost gone). Sprinkle the parsnips with sugar during the last 10 minutes of cooking.

Potato Cakes
(makes 8)

What ya need:

3 cups mashed potatoes (use leftovers from "Old-Fashioned Mashed Potatoes")

1 egg

1 heaping tablespoon flour

¼ cup finely chopped onion

vegetable oil

¼ cup butter (plus extra if needed)

flour

What ya do:

Mix potatoes and egg. Add flour and mix well. Add the onion and mix again. Pour oil into a frying pan, enough to cover the bottom of the pan, and then add the butter to melt in the oil. Heat them on high, then lower the heat to medium when the oil and butter start to sizzle. Pat potato mixture into balls and flatten into cakes. Roll them in the flour. Fry the cakes and turn after about 5 minutes. Continue flipping potato cakes every 4-5 minutes until both sides are a deep golden brown. Add extra oil and butter as needed to keep moisture in the pan while frying.

Squash Blooms

(serves 1)

What ya need:

2 large squash blooms

cornmeal

butter

salt to taste

What ya do:

Get the largest blooms from a squash vine. Wash the blooms, then roll in cornmeal to coat. Fry brown in butter, adding salt to your taste.

Tip: When picking flowers off the squash plant, be careful not to overpick, or the plant will start to make its buds taste bitter.

Yellow Crookneck Squash

(serves 4)

What ya need:

4 squash

salt to taste

pepper to taste

2 handfuls cornmeal

2 handfuls flour

$\frac{1}{2}$ cup butter

$\frac{1}{4}$ cup oil

1 onion, chopped (optional)

1 teaspoon sugar

What ya do:

Wash squash and cut into $\frac{1}{4}$-inch slices in a bowl. Salt and pepper the slices, hand-turning them to get all sides dusted. Dump cornmeal and flour in with the slices. Hand-toss the slices in the meal and flour to well-coat each piece. Melt butter and oil on medium-high heat in a skillet and add the squash. (If butter and oil cook down too low, add only more vegetable oil to continue frying in.

Adding more butter would make the squash too salty.)
As the squash browns, turn it to get all sides and pieces
even. Add the onion, if desired, and sprinkle on the
sugar. Continue turning and cooking squash until golden
brown.

Mountain Munchies

Fried Apple Pies

(serves 8-10)

What ya need:

1 1/2 cups dried apples

2/3 cup water

1/3 cup apple butter

1 1/2 tablespoons sugar

2 cups self-rising flour, sifted

1/2 cup buttermilk

1/3 cup lard or shortening

lard for frying

What ya do:

Soak dried apples overnight. Slow-boil the apples in water until tender, about 45 minutes. Add apple butter and sugar after the apples are done. Set aside.

Combine flour, buttermilk, and lard to make the pastry dough. Roll out your dough thin. Cut a piece of dough large enough to fold over the amount of apples you want inside one pie. Fold the dough over apples and seal edges tight with a fork. Put pie in a frying pan with lard and fry both sides till brown. (Add more lard for frying as needed.)

Tip: To dry your own apples, wash, peel, and core the fresh fruit. Cut the apples into thin slices, then put them on a dry rack in a place where they can get heat. When the slices have dried (in about 2 weeks) put them in a container with a tight lid.

Salt Lick Surprise

Mountain children were a hearty bunch. I can attest to it. We swallowed more pond water from the swimming hole and inadvertently downed more bugs during evening fire-fly chases than the average kid. We were immune to ordinary germs. Had to be, as the barnyard and the fields were our playground.

I remember one particular outdoor treat that my brothers and I loved: salty apples. Picked straight from the tree, green mountain apples held a pucker that could curl your tongue. But we learned that sprinkling on salt was a tasty way to cut the tang. The salt blocks in my daddy's pasture were set off the ground on stands with open bottoms. Since the cows licked off the tops of the blocks, my brothers and I saw no harm in rubbing our apples on the undersides. We got salty apples without having to stop playing and run all the way back to the house for a shaker!

Blackberry Cobbler
(serves 4-6)

What ya need:

1 1/4 cups sifted flour

1/2 cup shortening

1/2 cup buttermilk

1 quart fresh blackberries

1/2 cup sugar

What ya do:

Combine flour, shortening, and buttermilk to make dough.
Divide in half. Roll out on a floured surface to make two
layers. Put the first layer in the bottom and sides of a
9 x 9 baking dish. Put the berries in a pot. Fill the pot
with water until it is just visible beneath the blackberries.
Boil till the berries are done (when they are soft but not
mushed looking). Now you add the sugar and boil until
the water reaches a thick syrup. Then pour over dough.
Top with the second layer of dough. Bake in a 375-
degree oven until the dough is golden brown, about 40
minutes.

Blackberry Dumpling
(serves 6)

What ya need:

1 ½ pounds fresh blackberries

4 cups water

1 ½ cups sugar

biscuit dough (see "MeMa's Old-Timey Biscuits")

What ya do:

Low-boil blackberries (in just enough water to almost cover them) for about 20 minutes to allow the berry juices to seep out. Stir in the sugar and mix well. Bring back to a boil. Drop dough by the heaping spoonfuls into berries and juice. Simmer until the dough gets done, about 15 minutes.

Tasty Tidbit: Serve dumplings hot with real cream. Yum!

Black Walnut Cake
(serves 12)

What ya need:

3 cups plain flour

1/2 teaspoon baking powder

1/2 teaspoon salt

1/2 pound butter

1/2 cup lard or shortening

1 1/2 cups sugar

1 cup brown sugar

6 eggs

1 cup milk

1 cup chopped walnuts

What ya do:

Sift together flour, baking powder, and salt. Set aside.
Cream together the butter, lard, sugar, and brown sugar.
Add the eggs one at a time. Beat each egg as it is added
to the batter. Then pour in the flour mixture along with
the milk. Beat well. Finally, add the walnuts and mix a final
time. Pour into a Bundt pan and bake at 325 degrees for
about 1 hour.

Bread Pudding
(serves 4-6)

What ya need:

2½ cups crumbled biscuits (see "MeMa's
      Old-Timey Biscuits")

1½ cups milk

½ cup sugar

2 eggs

½ teaspoon vanilla

What ya do:

Pour crumbled biscuits into a 1-quart loaf baking dish
(greased). In a bowl, combine milk, sugar, and eggs, then
beat well. Mix in the vanilla and pour over the bread.
Bake at 350 degrees for about 45 minutes.

Chocolate Pie With Meringue Topping
(serves 6)

What ya need:

5 tablespoons cocoa

2 tablespoons plain flour

1 cup sugar

1/4 teaspoon salt

4 egg yolks (set whites aside to make meringue)

1 cup condensed milk

1 teaspoon vanilla

1 tablespoon butter

1 baked pie shell (see "Pie Crust")

meringue (see "Meringue Topping")

What ya do:

Mix together the cocoa, flour, sugar, and salt. Beat the egg yolks well in a separate bowl, then add them to the cocoa mixture. Add in milk and vanilla, then mix well. Pour the mixture into a pot and add butter. Cook over medium heat, stirring constantly. Bring to a rolling boil. Remove from heat and pour into the pie shell. Let cool. Top with meringue or whipped cream.

135

Egg Custard Pie

(serves 6)

What ya need:

¹/₄ pound butter

2 cups sugar

¹/₄ teaspoon salt

4 eggs

3 tablespoons plain flour

1 cup condensed milk

1 teaspoon vanilla

1 unbaked pie shell (see "Pie Crust")

nutmeg

What ya do:

Cream together the butter, sugar, salt, and eggs, adding the eggs one at a time. Mix in flour, milk, and vanilla, and beat well. Pour into the pie shell and sprinkle with nutmeg. Bake at 350 degrees for 40-50 minutes.

Meringue Topping

What ya need:

4 egg whites

1 tablespoon sugar

What ya do:

Beat egg whites and sugar till stiff. Spread over a pie and bake in the oven until meringue is golden brown.

Molasses and Apple Butter Cake
(serves 12)

What ya need:
2 cups plain flour

1/3 teaspoon salt

1/4 teaspoon ground cloves

1/2 teaspoon cinnamon

1/2 teaspoon ginger

1/8 teaspoon nutmeg

2 tablespoons baking powder

1/2 teaspoon baking soda

3/4 cup molasses

1/4 cup butter

2 eggs

3/4 cup buttermilk

apple butter (for layer filling and topping)

What ya do:
Sift together the flour, salt, cloves, cinnamon, ginger, nutmeg, baking powder, and soda. Set aside. In another bowl, mix the molasses and butter. Add the eggs to the molasses mixture and beat thoroughly. Then add in the dry

ingredients plus the buttermilk. Pour the batter into 6 separate greased and floured 8-inch cake pans to make thin layers. Bake layers at 350 degrees for approximately 20 minutes. When a toothpick inserted in the center of each layer comes out clean, the layers are done. Remove cakes from the oven and while warm, stack the layers with apple butter spread between them. Top the cake with apple butter as well.

Tasty Tidbit: Delicious served warm but tastes even better the next day after the apple butter has seeped into the layers.

A Molassey Boil

Fall was an exciting time up on the mountain. Crisp days brought not only color, but also the excitement of harvest and the indulgence of our childhood sweet tooths during the gathering for the molassey boil.

We grew our own sugar cane for molasses each year—there came a time we had to, as sugar was rationed in World War II. It was cheaper and easier to grow our own sugar cane and use the molasses as a natural sweetener than to travel all the way to the store to fight over a smidgen of the expensive white stuff.

Us and everybody else around would haul sugar cane by horse-drawn wagon to a neighbor's house. There a horse tethered to a long pole attached to the grinder walked circles all day, grinding the juice from long stalks hand-fed into the animal-powered machine. We then boiled the juice in long vats heated by an open flame. Folks took turns watching the liquid and keeping the top skimmed.

The neighborhood made molasses 24 hours a day

until everyone's cane was converted to the rich, dark syrup. What a grand time for the young people it was, coming together to play all night long under the stars and the sweet smells of the molassey boil.

Molasses Cookies
(makes 12-15)

What ya need:

2½ cups flour

1 teaspoon baking soda

¼ teaspoon salt

½ cup lard or shortening

1 cup molasses

1 egg

½ cup water

What ya do:

Sift together the flour, soda, and salt. Set aside. In another bowl, combine the lard, molasses, and egg. Beat well and add to the flour mixture, along with the water. Drop by the tablespoonful onto an ungreased baking sheet. Bake at 375 degrees for 8-10 minutes.

Oatmeal Cookies
(makes about 2 dozen)

What ya need:

1 cup butter

1 ½ cups brown sugar

3 eggs

2 teaspoons vanilla

4 cups uncooked oatmeal

1 cup lard or shortening

3 cups plain flour

½ teaspoon baking soda

1 teaspoon baking powder

What ya do:

Combine the butter, brown sugar, eggs, vanilla, oatmeal, and lard. Mix with hands, then knead in the flour, baking soda, and baking powder. Drop 1 tablespoon of dough per cookie onto an ungreased baking sheet. Bake at 350 degrees for about 10-15 minutes.

Filling Up the Tick

Alongside the harvesting and the molassey boils, buck-wheat-threshing time arrived. While grown-ups tended threshing machines, we children grabbed the ticks from our beds and headed for the fields to join them.

Dumping the worn-out straw from the previous year, we'd pile new buckwheat straw into the hand-sewn sacks. This was before we got mattresses in the country to sleep on, and a lumpy tick, if you stuffed it wrong, was just too bad—whatever you ended up with had to last until threshing time came back around the following year.

Peach Cobbler

(serves 6)

What ya need:

4 tablespoons butter

3/4 cup self-rising flour

3/4 cup sugar

1/2 cup milk

1/4 cup water

2 cups peaches (cut into medium-small chunks)

What ya do:

Put the butter in an 8 x 8 pan and melt in the oven. Mix the flour, sugar, milk, and water in a bowl. Beat the batter till smooth. Pour the peaches in the melted butter and coat them with the batter. Bake at 375 degrees for 30-40 minutes. The batter should be golden, and a tooth-pick should come out clean when inserted into it.

Tasty Tidbit: Substitute peaches with any fruit for a cobbler of your choice.

Pie Crust
(makes two 9-inch crusts)

What ya need:
2 cups self-rising flour, sifted
$1/3$ cup shortening
$1/2$ cup buttermilk

What ya do:
Measure sifted flour into a bowl, make a well in the center, and add the shortening and buttermilk. Blend until dough forms a ball. On a floured surface, roll out the dough to $1\frac{1}{2}$ inches larger than the pie pan. When well flattened, trim the dough another inch, and then place it in the pan. Roll the extra $1/2$ inch of dough under the edges of the pan. Bake at 400 degrees until slightly brown (about 15 minutes).

Popcorn Balls
(makes about 8-10)

What ya need:

2 tablespoons butter

1 cup sugar

$\frac{1}{2}$ cup water

$\frac{1}{2}$ cup molasses

1 teaspoon vinegar

$\frac{1}{2}$ teaspoon baking soda

2 quarts of popped corn

What ya do:

Mix and heat the butter, sugar, water, and molasses. Add in the vinegar and boil. The mixture is finished boiling when a drop of it into cold water forms a hard ball. Remove from heat and add the baking soda. Beat for 30 seconds. Pour the mixture over a bowl of popped corn and mix well. Grease hands with butter and shape the mixture into balls.

Pumpkin Pie

(serves 6)

What ya need:

1 sugar pumpkin (a small pie pumpkin)

2 eggs

1 cup cream

1/2 cup plain flour

3/4 cup sugar

1/2 teaspoon salt

1 teaspoon cinnamon

1/2 teaspoon nutmeg

1/2 teaspoon ginger

1 unbaked pie shell (see "Pie Crust")

whipped cream

What ya do:

Go to the field and get your pumpkin. Wash it well, then cut it in half. Remove the seeds and slice down the outside to remove the shell as well. Cut the pumpkin into small chunks and cook in a little water until done. Mash up the pumpkin till smooth, about 2 cups' worth. Add in the eggs and cream. In a separate bowl, mix the flour, sugar, salt, cinnamon, nutmeg, and ginger. Combine with the pumpkin mixture and beat well. Pour into the pie shell and bake at 400 degrees for 45 minutes. Top with whipped cream before serving.

Rhubarb Pie

(serves 6)

What ya need:

unbaked pie shell (see "Pie Crust")

1 ½ cups sugar

2 heaping tablespoons plain flour

⅓ teaspoon salt

4 cups rhubarb, finely cut

1 tablespoon butter

What ya do:

Prepare the pie crust, making enough dough to create a lattice top for the pie. Mix together the sugar, flour, and salt. Then add in the rhubarb. Pour into the pie shell, dot with butter, and lay on your lattice strips in a crisscross pattern. Bake at 375 degrees for about 40 minutes.

Sugar Cookies
(makes about 20)

What ya need:

2 cups unsifted flour

1 teaspoon baking soda

$1/3$ teaspoon salt

$1/2$ cup butter

1 cup brown sugar

2 eggs

$3/4$ cup buttermilk

$1/2$ teaspoon vanilla

What ya do:

Combine flour, baking soda, and salt. Set aside. In a separate bowl, mix the butter and brown sugar. Beat in the eggs gradually, then stir in the dry ingredients plus the buttermilk and vanilla. Drop by the tablespoonful onto a greased baking sheet. Flatten each cookie, and bake at 375 degrees for 8-10 minutes.

151

Snow Cream, Turkeys, and Blue Ridge Mountain Winters

A Blue Ridge Mountain winter can be a fickle thing these days. Snow comes now and then with a hint of surprise. It's not just a given like when I was growing up—then it was part of the expected seasonal cycle, like red and gold leaves marking fall or Grandma feeding us chicken soup with our sniffles. Winters just seemed colder back then, pure and simple. It'd start snowing before Christmas and we wouldn't see the ground again till spring of the following year.

Over-your-head drifts posed a special challenge around our bottom-of-the-hill homeplace, and animals got locked up tight in their coops or barns when a storm came upon us. But I remember one year, we left Mama's turkeys outside by accident. She saw them out there, three miserable fowls in a huddle by the fence, but the storm blew too hard to go save them. Figuring turkeys had at least a small lick of sense and could find their way across the yard to their coop proved too much of an assumption. In the morning, Mama checked the chicken house, and the turkeys weren't home. Tracing back to the scene of the last sighting, Mama found her turkeys in the exact same spot, the snow drifting over top of them and forming their own cozy tunnel. They were toasty warm in there, but Mama dug them out anyway and put them where they were supposed to be.

I wouldn't recommend making snow cream from the same patch of snow your barnyard critters have bedded down in, but if you've got a fresh, clean batch handy, all you need for this winter treat is milk, sugar, and vanilla. Mix the ingredients with your snow and set it back outside to refreeze. You don't have to venture far from your front door in a snowdrift to taste the pleasant sweetness of winter.

Vanilla Wafer Pudding
(serves 6-8)

What ya need:

1/2 cup sugar

3 tablespoons plain flour

2 egg yolks

2 tablespoons butter

1 teaspoon vanilla

1 cup milk

butter

vanilla wafers

1 very, very thin-sliced banana (optional)

What ya do:

Mix sugar, flour, egg yolks, butter, vanilla, and milk; then bring to a boil on the stove, stirring constantly, until the pudding is thick. Remove from heat. Grease a baking dish with butter and line the bottom of the dish with vanilla wafers. Cover the wafers with banana slices, then spoon the pudding over top. Continue layering wafers, banana, and pudding until the ingredients are gone. Place in the refrigerator to chill.

Yellow Cake With Hot Chocolate
(serves 15)

What ya need:

1 cup lard or shortening

2 cups sugar

3 cups plain flour

2 1/2 teaspoons baking powder

1/2 teaspoon salt

4 eggs

1 cup milk

1 1/2 teaspoons vanilla

What ya do:

Mix lard and sugar. In another bowl, sift together the flour, baking powder, and salt. Add eggs to the lard and sugar mixture and beat well. Gradually add the flour mixture along with the milk and vanilla to the lard and sugar mixture. Pour the batter into a sheet cake pan and bake at 350 degrees for 25-30 minutes.

Hot Chocolate Topping

Prepare the chocolate filling from "Chocolate Pie With Meringue Topping." Pour over individual slices of yellow cake.

155

Zucchini Pound Cake
(serves 12)

What ya need:

3 cups plain flour

2 teaspoons baking powder

1 teaspoon baking soda

$\frac{1}{2}$ teaspoon salt

$\frac{1}{2}$ teaspoon cinnamon

$\frac{1}{2}$ teaspoon nutmeg

4 eggs

3 cups sugar

$1\frac{1}{2}$ cups lard

3 cups zucchini, finely chopped

$\frac{2}{3}$ cup chopped walnuts

What ya do:

Sift together the flour, baking powder, baking soda, salt, cinnamon, and nutmeg. Set aside. Beat eggs in another bowl till foamy and set them aside. In a third bowl, mix sugar and lard until it's fluffy. Combine eggs with sugar and lard. Add in the zucchini, followed by the flour mixture. Mix all the ingredients well. Throw in the walnuts and bake the batter in a tube cake pan at 300 degrees for 1-1 1/2 hours.

For Medicinal Purposes—Really!

Folks in the country were a long ways off from the doctor, and in most cases, home remedies were the rule rather than the exception. Here are some of the more common concoctions my mother used when I was a child. While we grew up healthy and strong on home medicine, we recommend you check with your own doctor before trying any of these treatments. Not everyone has the constitution to gulp down some turpentine and feel the better for it!

Baked Onion Poultice (good for chest colds)
Take one large baked onion and break it apart. Put the pieces in a zippered plastic bag, then place on chest.

Catnip Tea (good for colic)
Pick and wash your catnip. Then put it in a pot and boil with a little water. Give 1 teaspoon to the colicky child.

Chicken Broth (good for sick stomach)
Boil chicken meat until the water has turned brothy. Drink the broth to settle an upset stomach.

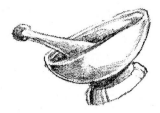

Turpentine and Sugar (good for lumbago)
Take a tablespoon of sugar and scatter 5 drops of turpentine over it. Eat.

Smoke in the Ear (good for an earache)
Take in a big lungful of pipe or cigar smoke and gently blow it into the ear of the hurting person for soothing.

Cabbage Leaves (good for infections)
Wrap a raw cabbage leaf around the infected area. It draws the fever out of the skin.

Whiskey and Honey (good for anything—just plain good!)
Mix ⅓ glass of whiskey with 1 teaspoon of honey and drink. Repeat. And repeat. In fact, repeat as many times as needed until the ailment disappears—or you just don't remember what was wrong in the first place!

Oh, By the Way . . .

Delving deep into the Virginia mountains and old-timey cooking for this project, it was fun for the Southerner in me to hear another take on some of the recipes. One of the most humorous tales to come out of the recipe testers' kitchens was this take from the Yankee in our family, a little Italian gal from Jersey who was unfamiliar with Mackerel and Eggs for breakfast. . . .

"As God is my witness, I'll never be hungry again!" Such a powerful statement sworn aloud by a battered and near broken woman as she raised one clenched fist up to the heavens while the other beat down upon the hard red clay of Georgia.

Miss Scarlett was lucky she had radishes and was not over to my house for dinner the other night.

I hate fish. I do. I hate the smell of fish, the look of fish, the texture of fish, the delicate way it has to be cooked and the fact that if it is not handled properly in the kitchen, it will kill your entire family with salmonella.

Now let's make Mackerel and Eggs. Aside from my healthy disdain for fish, husband Glenn and I took the recipe to test for the book. First we called MeMa and asked her half tongue-in-cheek, how'd they get mackerel up in the mountains?

They got theirs in the general store where it was sold by can. MeMa recommended we do the same, as there is no mackerel up in the mountains.

This recipe is super easy—anyone old enough to operate the stove by himself can do it. So, I, and my fearful respect for fish, went into the back room to cruise the Internet while my husband (who actually likes fish) cooked it up in the kitchen undisturbed. But I watched from afar, morbidly curious.

Open can. Slosh in the mackerel and warm it up in your pan. Add some eggs, season to taste, and serve a scoop with your other breakfast vittles. Glenn followed the test recipe and put a serving in a bowl for himself. He carried it back to my hideout. He looked in the bowl. He looked at me. He tilted the bowl so I could see.

"Oh my God! It's gray!"

Yes, it will turn a shade of gray that will make you not want to eat it, even on a dare. But my husband loves and trusts his MeMa, having grown up big and tall on her cooking. He dug in. I flinched. He told me in all honesty and sincerity that it is delicious.

"It's better in a sandwich, though," he later confided in me as he ate his second helping. "The bread hides it."

—Terry Bane

Ordering Information

Invite others to crowd around the mountain supper table!

Share a bit of the Blue Ridge with your family and friends. *Making Do: How to Cook Like a Mountain MeMa* makes a wonderful gift for the cooks in your life (or those who'd just like a taste of anecdotal mountain nostalgia).

To order additional copies, visit our Web site to place your order directly, or call us at 336-315-6080 Mon.-Fri., 10 a.m. to 5 p.m. Special bulk discounts are available for offices, church organizations, family reunions, or any other group with a hearty appetite. See you at the supper table!

www.NeDeoPress.com

Notes

Notes

Printed in the United States
41731LVS00006B/76